Beginning ALGEBRA THINKING

Grades 3–4

Table of Contents

Notes to the Teacher..iii

Solutions vii

Number Patterns 1

Ratios and Tables..7

What's the Rule? 13

Number Puzzles 19

Mystery Numbers 25

Seesaw Balances...31

Linking Circles 37

Square Puzzles 43

Story Problems..49

Published by Ideal School Supply
an imprint of
Frank Schaffer Publications®

ideal
school supply

Authors: Shirley Hoogeboom, Judy Goodnow

Frank Schaffer Publications®

Ideal School Supply is an imprint of Frank Schaffer Publications.

Send all inquiries to:
Frank Schaffer Publications
3195 Wilson Drive NW
Grand Rapids, Michigan 49534

Beginning Algebra Thinking—grades 3–4

ISBN: 1-56451-095-6

5 6 7 8 9 10 PAT 09 08 07

This is one of two books designed to prepare students for thinking algebraically:

Beginning Algebra Thinking, Grades 3-4
Beginning Algebra Thinking, Grades 5-6

The National Council of Teachers of Mathematics (NCTM) stresses that by providing students with "informal algebraic experiences throughout the K-8 curriculum, they will develop confidence in using algebra to represent and solve problems." Many algebra students never understand that algebra is a problem-solving tool, because for them, algebra is merely a group of symbols to be manipulated. They don't see the relevance of algebra to their world. If, in the early grades, we can give students rich experiences with problem-solving strategies, and introduce them informally to equations, variables, and other algebraic concepts, they will build the foundation for understanding this powerful tool.

Each book presents 54 reproducible pages of problems—some designed to be solved using concrete manipulatives (cubes), some designed to be solved using a calculator, and some presented in story form. Solutions are provided, including sample algebraic expressions and equations.

Introduction to Beginning Algebra Thinking, Grades 3-4

This book provides an informal introduction to thinking algebraically, beginning with problems in which students use cubes to find solutions. Manipulating concrete objects gives students the opportunity to explore problems, trying out different solutions. Exploring problems in this way allows students to develop a visual image of the solution process, making it easier to solve the same problem in a more abstract context. Next, students solve the same type of problem using a calculator. The calculator is an important tool for students, allowing them to concentrate on the problem-solving process. Finally, the same type of problem is presented in a story problem format. It is helpful for students to solve the same type of problem in a variety of formats.

Students solve each type of problem using a problem-solving strategy or combination of strategies. These strategies include: acting out with objects, working backwards, making and using tables, making and using diagrams, making an organized list, guess and check, and using patterns.

These strategies help students learn to identify the unknown quantity (variable) of a problem, and to see the relationship of the unknown quantity to the other data in the problem. These thinking skills are crucial for translating word phrases into algebraic expressions and equations—essential steps in algebra. As machines become more efficient with symbol manipulation, the translation from words to symbols becomes a critical skill for our students to master. All of the activities in this book allow students to practice this translation process.

Using Beginning Algebra Thinking, Grades 3-4

Contents

This book contains eight sequences of problems. Each six-page sequence focuses on one type of problem. The first four pages present problems accompanied by a diagram on which students can move cubes to work out solutions. The fifth page presents problems of the same kind containing larger numbers. Students use a calculator to solve them. The sixth page presents problems of the same kind in story form.

After the eight sequences, there are six pages of mixed story problems. Problem types are mixed so that students will be challenged to think through the problems and identify strategies that will help solve them.

Suggestions for Classroom Use

The problems are sequenced according to level of difficulty within each section. If you find that a problem or section is too challenging for your students, or not challenging enough, you can modify it to meet their needs.

These problems can be used by students working in pairs or individually. Working together encourages students to talk about their thinking and their discoveries. It is beneficial for students to articulate their thinking and to hear how others may have solved the same problem in a different way. Encourage your students to share their ideas with other pairs of students, with other small groups, or with the whole class. You may want pairs of students to show how they solved a problem by using the overhead projector. This talking about the process helps students make mathematical connections and enriches their understanding.

You can use the section of mixed story problems in a variety of ways. After students have completed the problems in a section, you can have them do the additional problems on pages 49-54 that are the same type. You may want to wait until students have completed all the sequences. Then they can think about which problem-solving strategies are appropriate for each problem. Have students create their own story problems. Pairs can write problems and exchange them with another pair, without identifying the type of problem.

Materials

It is recommended that each student or pair of students have a pencil, 100 cubes (20 of five different colors) for the pages showing the cube icon, and a calculator for the pages showing the calculator icon. You can make copies of the problems for each student or pair of students.

Introducing the Problems

Go over the first problem in each sequence with the students before they begin work. Review the problem-solving strategies used in that sequence. Help the students identify what information they are looking for in the problem. Have them identify what information is known and what information is unknown.

You might want to make an overhead transparency of the page and present it on the overhead projector, using transparent colored tiles. After the students have worked out some of the problems, you may want to have them demonstrate their solution strategies on the overhead.

You may want to encourage your students to try writing algebraic expressions and equations for the problems. First, give them time to explore with the cubes, then talk about how they could translate the information or data in the problem into letters or symbols. Talk about a *variable*: *a letter, shape, or other symbol used to represent an unknown quantity*. Also talk about an *equation*: *a number sentence in which the expressions on both sides of the equal sign represent the same value*. The solution section shows ways in which students can write algebraic expressions and equations for the problems. Students may find other ways to write expressions and equations that are equally correct.

Following is a brief description of the types of problems in each of the eight sequences and the problem-solving strategies students can use to solve them.

Pages 1-6: Number Patterns

Strategies students can use: act out with objects, use a diagram, make and use a table, look for patterns, and use a calculator.

Students use cubes to represent the number of creatures on the first four trips of a submarine down into the sea. They record the numbers in a table. They look for a pattern in the numbers of cubes and in the numbers recorded in the table. They use the numerical pattern to predict how many creatures will be on the next submarine trip.

Students may be able to generalize a rule about the numerical pattern and then use the rule to predict the number of creatures in the next trip. In the first problem on page 1, for example, the pattern is an increase of two on each trip. It is most important that students be able to describe the pattern in their own words, but some students can try writing the rule as an algebraic expression. In this case the rule would be: $2n$, with n being the number of the trip.

Pages 7-12: Ratios and Tables

Strategies students can use: act out with objects, use a diagram, make and use a table, and use a calculator.

Students are given the names and numbers of two kinds of animals that are riding in the cars of a train. They are also given the total number of animals riding on the train. Students use cubes to represent the animals in each car, adding cubes as they add cars, until they reach the given total. The number of each kind of animal in each car remains constant, so the ratio remains the same between the totals for each animal as the number of cars increases. Students record the numbers of animals for one car, two cars, and so on. They use the cubes and numbers in the table to find out how many of each kind of animal is on the train. Students may be able to generalize a rule about the ratio between the two variables and the total.

In the first problem on page 7, the ratio between the variables is $1:2$. The students can try writing equations about information given: $F = n$ (number of cars filled), $C = 2n$, $F + C =$ Total.

Pages 13-18: What's the Rule?

Strategies students can use: act out with objects, use a diagram, make and use a table, guess and check, look for patterns, and use a calculator.

Students are given pairs of input numbers and output numbers for two machines. The numbers are given in a table. Students use cubes to act out the problems on diagrams of the machines. They can guess and check and also look for the pattern in the relationships between the numbers to help them find the secret rule (function) of each machine. Then they use the rules to complete the tables.

In the first problem on page 13, the difference between the input number and output number in each pair is $+ 4$. The students can try writing the rule as an algebraic expression. In this case the rule would be: $n + 4$, and n stands for the input number.

Pages 19-24: Number Puzzles

Strategies students can use: act out with objects, use a diagram, work backwards, and use a calculator.

Students begin with one known quantity, which is given at the end of the problem. They work backwards, using the clues for each unknown to find its value. They can use different-colored cubes to represent each thing, beginning with the known quantity.

The students can try writing equations for each clue. For example, equations for the clues in the first problem on page 19 could be: $Y = 2$, $B = Y + 5$, $O = B + 4$. An equation for the total could be: $Y + B + O = T$.

Pages 25-30: Mystery Numbers

Strategies students can use: act out with objects, use a diagram, guess and check, and use a calculator.

Students are given the total number of objects, the number of different colors, and clues about the number relationships between the colors. The variables are the unknown number of each color. Students will begin by guessing and checking. The students take the cubes and explore representing a color with different numbers of cubes. They look for all the ways they can solve the problem. As they make a list of their answers, they will begin to see relationships between the numbers.

The students can try writing the clues as algebraic expressions. For example, for the first problem on page 25, they can write: $P + D = 7$, $P = D + 1$.

Pages 31-36: Seesaw Balances

Strategies students can use: act out with objects, use a diagram, guess and check, make and use an organized list, and use a calculator.

A seesaw is a good model for introducing students to equations, because both sides must have the same mass (equal value) for it to balance. In these problems, each robot on the seesaw has a weight (represents a number). Robots that are the same have the same weight. Robots that are different have different weights. The total weight of robots on one side must equal the total weight of robots on the other side. Students are given the weight of one of the robots. They can take cubes equal to that weight. They can take an equal number of cubes to represent the weight of the robots on the other side, then arrange them to find out what each of the other robots could weigh. Recording in the list will help students to see whether all possible solutions have been found. They can also look for patterns in the relationships between the numbers in the list.

The students can try writing an equation for the variables. For example, the equation for finding the weights of robots in the first problem on page 31 could be: $A = B + C$; $A = 4$.

Pages 37-42: Linking Circles

Strategies students can use: act out with objects, use a diagram, use logical thinking, and use a calculator.

Students use logical reasoning skills as they sort out the different sections and intersections of the linking circles, which are Venn diagrams. For example, in the first problem on page 37, students will find out that circle A has two sections—one not shared and one shared with circle B; circle B has two sections—one not shared and one shared with circle A. Total values are given for a circle, which includes the intersection. Later problems include three interlocking circles, with circle B having two intersections. Students will need to think about these problems to understand how the intersections are subtracted from the totals to find values for a, b, and c.

Equations help to show how these problems are solved. To find the total, the equation for the first problem on page 37 is: $a + b + c = $ Total. Information is given in this problem for section c, so the variables are sections a and b. Equations for the variables are: $a = 8 - c$, and $b = 6 - c$.

Pages 43-48: Square Puzzles

Strategies students can use: act out with objects, use a diagram, make and use an organized list, and use a calculator.

In this sequence students act out the solution process using numbered squares of paper instead of cubes. First, students need to cut out and number the small squares of paper that they will need. Then they make an organized list of addends that make the sum given for the square puzzle. They use the list and the numbered pieces of paper to solve the puzzle. When solving the puzzles that have nine spaces in a square, students may gradually discover that the number in the center space is always the average of any three addends that make the given sum, or the sum divided by three.

Students can try writing equations to represent each column and row of a puzzle, or in each column, row, and main diagonal. For example, equations for the first problem on page 43 could be: $a + b + c = 12$, $a + d + f = 12$, $f + g + h = 12$, $c + e + h = 12$.

Solutions

These are sample solutions. Students may find other correct answers.

1
1. 10 crabs: the difference between trips is + 2; $2n$
2. 6 clams; the difference between trips is + 1; $n + 1$

2
1. 15 toads; the difference between trips is + 3; $3n$
2. 25 snails; the difference between trips is + 5; $5n$

3
1. 7 turtles; the difference between trips is − 2; $17 − 2n$
2. 4 snakes; the difference between trips is − 4; $24 − 4n$

4
1. 24 sharks; the difference between trips is + 5; $5n − 1$
2. 6 frogs; the difference between trips is − 4; $26 − 4n$

5
1. 63 worms; the difference between trips is + 6; $6n + 3$
2. 16 fish; the difference between trips is − 8; $96 − 8n$

6
1. 4 people; the difference between shows is − 7; $67 − 7n$
2. 57 riders; the difference between rides is + 7; $5n + 7$
3. 84 caps total; the difference between hours is + 4; $4n$

7
1. 4 frogs, 8 crickets; $F = n$ (the number of cars); $C = 2n$; $F + C = 12$
2. 12 toads, 8 bees; $Td = 3n$; $B = 2n$; $Td + B = 20$

8
1. 20 robins, 4 beetles; $R = 5n$; $B = n$; $R + B = $ Total; $T = 24$
2. 10 frogs, 20 grasshoppers; $F = 2n$; $G = 4n$; $F + G = 30$

9
1. 15 slugs, 10 bugs; $S = 3n$; $B = 2n$; $S + B = 25$
2. 8 worms, 20 ants; $W = 2n$; $A = 5n$; $W + A = 28$

10
1. 20 flies, 12 mice; $F = 5n$; $M = 3n$; $F + M = 32$
2. 15 caterpillars, 20 moths; $C = 3n$; $M = 4n$; $C + M = 35$

11
1. 48 crawlers, 32 snails; $C = 6n$; $S = 4n$; $C + S = 80$
2. 42 lizards, 35 frogs; $L = 6n$; $F = 5n$; $L + F = 77$

12
1. Rabbit will reach 30 feet. $R = 6n$; $T = 2n$; $T = 10$
2. 36 spinners, total 108 things; $S = 4n$; $G = 8n$; $G = 72$; $S + G = $ Total
3. 24 drumbeaters, 72 whistletoots; $D = 3n$; $W = 9n$; $D + W = 96$

13
1. Rule: + 4; $n + 4$ ($n = $ the input number)
2. Rule: − 3; $n − 3$

14
1. Rule: + 7; $n + 7$ 2. Rule: − 6; $n − 6$

15
1. Rule: + 9; $n + 9$ 2. Rule: x 2; $2n$

16
1. Rule: x 3; $3n$ 2. Rule: ÷ 2; $n ÷ 2$

17
1. Rule: x 5; $5n$ 2. Rule: ÷ 3; $n ÷ 3$

18
1. 10 tickets; $n + 4$ 2. Floor 16; $n − 5$
3. 100 tubs; $5n$

19
1. 2 yellow, 7 blue, 11 orange, Total = 20; $Y = 2$; $B = Y + 5$; $O = B + 4$; $T = 20$

20
2. 7 red, 7 green , 13 pink, Total = 27; $R = 7$, $G = R$, $P = G + 6$, $T = 27$

20
1. 8 green, 5 white, 17 orange, Total = 30; $G = 8$, $W = G − 3$, $O = W + 12$, $T = 30$
2. 6 blue, 16 yellow, 12 green, Total = 34; $B = 6$, $Y = B + 10$, $G = Y − 4$, $T = 34$

21
1. 3 white, 8 yellow, 6 green, 6 orange, Total = 23; $W = 3$, $Y = W + 5$, $G = Y − 2$, $O = G$, $T = 23$
2. 4 red, 3 pink, 11 blue, 7 brown, Total = 25; $R = 4$, $P = R − 1$, $Bl = P + 8$, $Br = Bl − 4$, $T = 25$

22
1. 2 red, 4 yellow, 10 black, 8 orange, Total = 24; $R = 2$, $Y = 2R$, $Bl = Y + 6$, $O = Bl − 2$, $T = 24$
2. 5 green, 2 blue, 8 purple, 14 white, Total = 29; $G = 5$, $Blue = G − 3$, $P = 4B$, $W = P + 6$, $T = 29$

23
1. 10 white, 22 red, 66 blue, 50 green, Total = 148; $W = 10$, $R = W + 12$, $Bl = 3R$, $G = Blu − 16$, $T = 148$
2. 15 yellow, 60 purple, 90 orange, 63 brown, Total = 228; $Y = 15$, $P = 4Y$, $O = P + 30$, $B = O − 27$, $T = 228$

24
1. 85 bags: 10 bags of burgers, 25 bags of berry pies, 50 bags of honey cakes; $B = 10$; $BP = B + 15$; $HC = 2BP$; $B + BP + HC = $ Total
2. 43 animals: 6 pigs, 9 sheep, 7 goats, 21 rabbits; $P = 6$; $S = P + 6$; $G = S − 2$; $R = 3G$; $P + S + G + R = $ Total
3. There's Bears = 5, Cookie Cottage = 13, Toy Fair = 11, T-Shirt Madness = 8, Pizza Stop = 24; $TB = 5$; $CC = TB + 8$; $TF = CC − 2$; $TS = TF − 3$

25
1. 4 pigs, 3 dogs; $P + D = 7$; $P = D + 1$
2. 8 cats, 2 goats; $C + G = 10$; $C = G + 6$

26
1. 6 birds, 9 mice; $B + M = 15$; $B = M − 3$
2. 12 rabbits, 8 turtles; $R + T = 20$; $T = R − 4$

27
1. 7 moles, 5 lizards, 4 skunks; $M + L + S = 16$; $M = L + 2$; $S = L − 1$
2. 10 possums, 10 snakes, 4 raccoons; $P + R + S = 24$; $P = S$; $R = S − 6$

28
1. 12 dogs, 9 cats, 7 rabbits; $D + C + R = 28$; $D = C + 3$; $R = C − 2$
2. 15 goats, 10 pigs, 7 turtles; $G + P + T = 32$; $G = P + 5$; $T = P − 3$

29
1. 16 birds, 24 mice, 15 lizards; $B + M + L = 55$; $M = B + 8$; $L = B − 1$
2. 23 snakes, 30 possums, 17 moles; $S + P + M = 70$; $P = S + 7$; $M = S − 6$

30
1. 8 monsters, 2 witches, 2 ghosts; $M + W + G = 12$; $W = M − 6$; $W = G$
2. 9 flies, 6 mosquitoes, 10 moths; $F + Mos + Mot = 25$; $F = Mos + 3$; $Mos = Mot − 4$
3. 12 green, 10 red, 8 orange; $G + R + O = 30$; $G = R + 2$; $O = R − 2$

31

A ⬠	B ◇	C ◯
1. 4	1	3
4	3	1

$A = B + C;\ A = 4$

2. 7	1	6
7	2	5
7	3	4
7	4	3
7	5	2
7	6	1

$A = B + C;\ A = 7$

32

A ▢	B ◯	C ▯
1. 3	1	5
3	2	4
3	4	2
3	5	1

$2A = B + C;\ A = 3$

2. 5	1	9
5	2	8
5	3	7
5	4	6
5	6	4
5	7	3
5	8	2
5	9	1

$2A = B + C;\ A = 5$

33

A ◯	B ▭	C ⬡
1. 1	8	3
2	7	3
4	5	3
5	4	3
7	2	3
8	1	3

$A + B = 3C;\ C = 3$

2. 1	11	4
2	10	4
3	9	4
5	7	4
7	5	4
9	3	4
10	2	4
11	1	4

$A + B = 3C;\ C = 4$

34

A ⬠	B ▭	C △
1. 5	1	7
5	3	6
5	7	4
5	9	3
5	11	2
5	13	1

$3A = B + 2C;\ A = 5$

2. 6	2	8
6	4	7
6	8	5
6	10	4
6	12	3
6	14	2
6	16	1

$3A = B + 2C;\ A = 6$

35

A ◯	B ⬡	C ▢
1. 9	1	13
9	3	12
9	5	11
9	7	10
9	11	8
9	13	7
9	15	6
9	17	5
9	19	4
9	21	3
9	23	2
9	25	1

$3A = B + 2C;\ A = 9$

A ◯	B ⬡	C ▢
2. 8	2	11
8	4	10
8	6	9
8	10	7
8	12	6
8	14	5
8	16	4
8	18	3
8	20	2
8	22	1

$3A = B + 2C;\ A = 8$

36

Clown	Plane	Robot
1. 3	1	5
3	2	4
3	4	2
3	5	1

$2C = P + R;\ C = 3$

Book	Animal	Lunch
2. 10	1	18
10	2	16
10	3	14
10	4	12
10	6	8
10	7	6
10	8	4
10	9	2

$2B = 2A + L;\ B = 10$

Magnet	Pencil	Eraser
3. 10	1	14
10	2	13
10	3	12
10	4	11
10	6	9
10	7	8
10	8	7
10	9	6
10	11	4
10	12	3
10	13	2
10	14	1

$3M = 2P + 2E;\ M = 10$

37

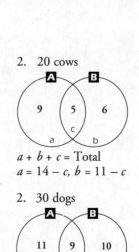

1. 12 horses

$a + b + c = \text{Total}$
$a = 8 - c,\ b = 6 - c$

2. 20 cows

$a + b + c = \text{Total}$
$a = 14 - c,\ b = 11 - c$

38

1. 24 cats

$a + b + c = \text{Total}$
$a = 17 - c,\ b = 14 - c$

2. 30 dogs

$a + b + c = \text{Total}$
$a = 20 - c,\ b = 19 - c$

39

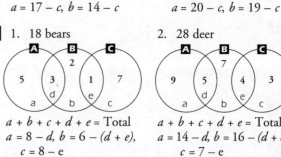

1. 18 bears

$a + b + c + d + e = \text{Total}$
$a = 8 - d,\ b = 6 - (d + e),$
$c = 8 - e$

2. 28 deer

$a + b + c + d + e = \text{Total}$
$a = 14 - d,\ b = 16 - (d + e),$
$c = 7 - e$

40

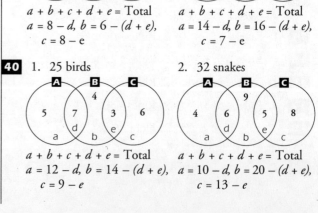

1. 25 birds

$a + b + c + d + e = \text{Total}$
$a = 12 - d,\ b = 14 - (d + e),$
$c = 9 - e$

2. 32 snakes

$a + b + c + d + e = \text{Total}$
$a = 10 - d,\ b = 20 - (d + e),$
$c = 13 - e$

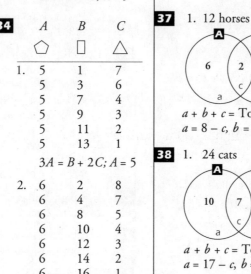
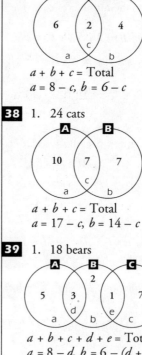

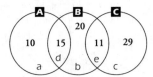

41 1. 85 horses

a + b + c + d + e = Total; a = 25 − d, b = 46 − (d + e), c = 40 − e

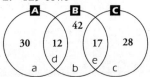

2. 129 cows

a + b + c + d + e = Total
a = 42 − d, b = 71 − (d + e), c = 45 − e

42 1. 40 children   2. 27 people

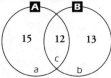 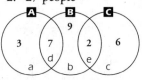

a + b + c = Total   a + b + c + e = Total
a = 27 − c, b = 25 − c   a = 10 − d, b = 18 − (d + e),
                          c = 8 − e

3. 56 robotrons

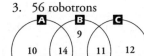

a + b + c + d + e = Total
a = 24 − d, b = 34 − (d + e), c = 23 − e

43 1.

Sum of 12		
8	3	1
7	4	1
7	3	2
6	5	1
6	4	2
5	4	3

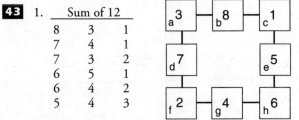

a + b + c = 12, a + d + f = 12, f + g + h = 12, c + e + h = 12

2.

Sum of 14		
8	5	1
8	4	2
7	6	1
7	5	2
7	4	3
6	5	3

a4 b2 c8 / d3 e5 / f7 g6 h1

44 1.

a 9	b 4	c 3
d 5		e 7
f 2	g 8	h 6

2.

a 8	b 3	c 7
d 6		e 2
f 4	g 5	h 9

45 1.

a 6	b 7	c 2
d 1	e 5	f 9
g 8	h 3	i 4

2.

a 9	b 2	c 7
d 4	e 6	f 8
g 5	h 10	i 3

b + e + h = 15, c + f + i = 15,
a + b + c = 15, d + e + f = 15,
a + e + i = 15, c + e + g = 15,
g + h + i = 15, a + d + g = 15

46 1.

a 1	b 8	c 3
d 6	e 4	f 2
g 5	h 0	i 7

2.

a 5	b 12	c 4
d 6	e 7	f 8
g 10	h 2	i 9

47 1.

a 7	b 21	c 5
d 9	e 11	f 13
g 17	h 1	i 15

or

a 20	b 1	c 12
d 3	e 11	f 19
g 10	h 21	i 2

2.

a 40	b 5	c 30
d 15	e 25	f 35
g 20	h 45	i 10

48 1.

a 9	b 8	c 3
d 5		e 7
f 6	g 4	h 10

2.

a 6	b 13	c 5
d 7	e 8	f 9
g 11	h 3	i 10

3.

a 18	b 11	c 16
d 13	e 15	f 17
g 14	h 19	i 12

49 1. 55 bags of popcorn; $6n + 7$
2. 24 alligoats and 48 crocodogs; $A = 4n$; $C = 8n$; $A + C = 72$
3. 8 people on surfboards, 13 people building sand castles, 26 people swimming, 16 people playing ball; $S = 8$, $SC = S + 5$; $SW = 2SC$, $B = SW - 10$

50 1. 20 swimming, 5 diving, 10 water polo, 8 water safety; $S + D + WP + WS = 43$; $S = 4D$; $D = WP - 5$, $WP = WS + 2$
2. 66 bags of coins, 55 bags of bills; $C = 6n$, $B = 5n$, $C + B = 121$
3. 20 pairs of socks; the rule is the input number x 2; $2n$

51 1. 150 bags; $10n$ (n = the number of hours)
2.

a 12	b 27	c 6
d 9	e 15	f 21
g 24	h 3	i 18

3. 7 black, 9 brown, 3 white; $Bl + Br + W = 19$; $Br = Bl + 2$; $W = Br - 6$

52 1. 39 people; $S = 6$, $R = S + 6$, $H = R - 5$, $T = 2H$
2. 13 robots; the rule is the input number ÷ 2; $n ÷ 2$
3. 6 orange, 8 red, 10 yellow, 12 blue; $B + Y + O + R = 36$; $B = Y + 2$, $Y = R + 2$, $O = R - 2$

53 1.

Melon	Apple	Pear
15	1	13
15	2	11
15	3	9
15	4	7
15	6	3
15	7	1

2.

a 11	b 4	c 9
d 7		e 5
f 6	g 8	h 10

3. 43 students; $a + b + c$ = Total; $a = 30 - c$, $b = 25 - c$

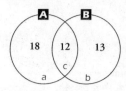

54 1. They have made 34 favors, so they have 2 more to make; $a + b + c + d + e$ = Total; $a = 14 - d$; $b = 20 - (d + e)$, $c = 11 - e$

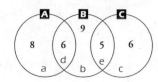

2.

Nutty Nuggets	Grand Slam	Dino Crunches
25	1	12
25	3	11
25	5	10
25	7	9
25	9	8
25	11	7
25	13	6
25	15	5
25	17	4
25	19	3
25	21	2
25	23	1

3. 8 stars, 6 planes; $P + S = 14$; $S = P + 2$

Use cubes and the tables to solve the problems.

1 On Monday, 2 crabs are in the Seahorse Sub on the first trip down into the sea. Four crabs are on the second trip, 6 crabs are on the third trip, and 8 crabs are on the fourth trip. If the pattern continues, how many crabs will be on the fifth trip?

Trip	Crabs
1	2
2	4
3	6
4	
5	

2 On Tuesday, 2 clams are in the sub on the first trip down, 3 clams are on the second trip, 4 clams are on the third trip, and 5 clams are on the fourth trip. If the pattern continues, how many clams will be on the fifth trip?

Trip	Clams
1	
2	
3	
4	
5	

Use cubes and the tables to solve the problems.

1 On Wednesday, 3 toads are in the Seahorse Sub on the first trip down, 6 toads are on the second trip, 9 toads are on the third trip, and 12 toads are on the fourth trip. If the pattern continues, how many toads will be on the fifth trip?

Trip	Toads

2 On Thursday, 5 snails are in the sub on the first trip down, 10 snails are on the second trip, 15 snails are on the third trip, and 20 snails are on the fourth trip. If the pattern continues, how many snails will be on the fifth trip?

Trip	Snails

 Beginning Algebra Thinking, Grades 3-4 • ©Ideal School Supply Company

Use cubes and the tables to solve the problems.

1 On Friday, 15 turtles are in the Seahorse Sub on the first trip down, 13 turtles are on the second trip, 11 turtles are on the third trip, and 9 turtles are on the fourth trip. If the pattern continues, how many turtles will be on the fifth trip?

Trip	Turtles

2 On Saturday, 20 snakes are in the sub on the first trip down, 16 snakes are on the second trip, 12 snakes are on the third trip, and 8 snakes are on the fourth trip. If the pattern continues, how many snakes will be on the fifth trip?

Trip	Snakes

Use cubes and the tables to solve the problems.

1 On Monday, 4 sharks are in the Seahorse Sub on the first trip down. Nine sharks are on the second trip, 14 sharks are on the third trip, and 19 sharks are on the fourth trip. If the pattern continues, how many sharks will be on the fifth trip?

Trip	Sharks

2 On Tuesday, 22 frogs are in the sub on the first trip down, 18 frogs are on the second trip, 14 frogs are on the third trip, and 10 frogs are on the fourth trip. If the pattern continues, how many frogs will be on the fifth trip?

Trip	Frogs

Use the tables and a calculator to solve the problems.

1 On Wednesday, 9 worms are in Seahorse Sub on the first trip down. Fifteen worms are on the second trip, 21 worms are on the third trip, and 27 worms are on the fourth trip. If the pattern continues, how many worms will be on the tenth trip?

Trip	Worms

2 On Thursday, 88 fish are in the sub on the first trip down, 80 fish are on the second trip, 72 fish are on the third trip, and 64 fish are on the fourth trip. If the pattern continues, how many fish will be on the tenth trip?

Trip	Fish

1 Word got around that "Hippo Invades Chicago" was a horrible show! There were 60 people at the first show. Only 53 people came to see the second show, 46 came to the third show, and 39 came to the fourth show. If the pattern continued, how many people came to see the ninth show?

2 Toshio and his friends rode the RollerRocket ride. There were 12 riders on the first ride, 17 on the second ride, 22 on the third ride, and 27 on the fourth ride. If the pattern continues, how many riders will there be on the tenth ride?

3 Crazy Caps is giving away free caps today! The sales people gave away 4 caps in the first hour, 8 caps in the second hour, 12 caps in the third hour, and 16 caps in the fourth hour. If the pattern continues, how many crazy caps will they give away in six hours?

Use cubes and the tables to solve the problems.

1 One frog and two crickets get onto the first car of Mole's train. Then one frog and two crickets get onto the second car. Frogs and crickets continue getting on Mole's train in the same way—one frog and two crickets to a car. When Mole counts 12 riders, he starts the train. How many frogs and how many crickets are on the train when it starts?

Cars	Frogs	Crickets	Total Riders
1	1	2	3
2	2	4	6

2 Three toads and two bees get onto the first car of Mole's train. Then three toads and two bees get onto the second car. Toads and bees continue getting on Mole's train in the same way—three toads and two bees to a car. When Mole counts 20 riders, he starts the train. How many toads and how many bees are on the train when it starts?

Cars	Toads	Bees	Total Riders

Use cubes and the tables to solve the problems.

1 Five robins and one beetle fly into the first car of Mole's train. Then five robins and one beetle fly into the second car. Robins and beetles continue flying into Mole's train in the same way—five robins and one beetle to a car. When Mole counts 24 riders, he starts the train. How many robins and how many beetles are on the train when it starts?

Cars	Robins	Beetles	Total Riders

2 Two frogs and four grasshoppers hop onto the first car of Mole's train. Then two frogs and four grasshoppers hop onto the second car. Frogs and grasshoppers continue hopping on Mole's train in the same way—two frogs and four grasshoppers to a car. When Mole counts 30 riders, he starts the train. How many frogs and how many grasshoppers are on the train when it starts?

Cars	Frogs	Grasshoppers	Total Riders

Use cubes and the tables to solve the problems.

1 Three slugs and two bugs crawl onto the first car of Mole's train. Then three slugs and two bugs crawl onto the second car. Slugs and bugs continue crawling onto Mole's train in the same way—three slugs and two bugs to a car. When Mole counts 25 riders, he blows the whistle. How many slugs and how many bugs are on the train when Mole blows the whistle?

Cars	Slugs	Bugs	Total Riders

2 Two worms and five ants crawl onto the first car of Mole's train. Then two worms and five ants crawl onto the second car. Worms and ants continue crawling onto Mole's train in the same way—two worms and five ants to a car. When Mole counts 28 riders, he starts the train. How many worms and how many ants are on the train when it starts?

Cars	Worms	Ants	Total Riders

Use cubes and the tables to solve the problems.

1 Five flies and three mice climb onto the first car of Mole's train. Then five flies and three mice climb onto the second car. Flies and mice continue getting on Mole's train in the same way—five flies and three mice to a car. When Mole counts 32 riders, he starts the train. How many flies and how many mice are on the train when it starts?

Cars	Flies	Mice	Total Riders

2 Three caterpillars and four moths get onto the first car of Mole's train. Then three caterpillars and four moths get onto the second car. Caterpillars and moths continue getting on Mole's train in the same way—three caterpillars and four moths to a car. When Mole counts 35 riders, he starts the train. How many caterpillars and how many moths are on the train when it starts?

Cars	Caterpillars	Moths	Total Riders

Use the tables and a calculator to solve the problems.

1 Six crawlers and four snails slip and slide onto the first car of Mole's train. Then six crawlers and four snails slip onto the second car. Crawlers and snails continue getting on Mole's train in the same way—six crawlers and four snails to a car. When there are 80 riders in the cars, Mole starts the train. How many crawlers and how many snails are on the train when it starts?

Cars	Crawlers	Snails	Total Riders

2 Six lizards and five frogs leap onto the first car of Mole's train. Then six lizards and five frogs leap onto the second car. Lizards and frogs continue getting on Mole's train in the same way—six lizards and five frogs to a car. When Mole counts 77 riders in the cars, he blows the whistle. How many lizards and how many frogs are on the train when Mole blows the whistle?

Cars	Lizards	Frogs	Total Riders

1 Turtle and Rabbit are ready for the race! They both have new batteries! Ready, set, go! Turtle moves ahead two feet in the first minute, while Rabbit moves forward six feet. Turtle moves ahead two more feet in the second minute, while Rabbit moves ahead another six feet. If Turtle and Rabbit keep moving like that, where will Rabbit be when Turtle reaches 10 feet?

2 Mari and Josh helped set up the gym for Family Night. They put four spinners and eight game markers on each table. There are 72 game markers on the tables. How many spinners are on the tables? How many things are on the tables all together?

3 Dr. Hornblower looks for rare birds in Fantastic Forest. Today she is amazed to discover three drumbeaters and nine whistletoots in each tree. She leaves the forest after counting 96 birds. How many drumbeaters and whistletoots has she discovered?

What's the Rule? - 1

Each machine has a secret rule.
Use cubes and the table to help find each secret rule.
Finish the table.

1

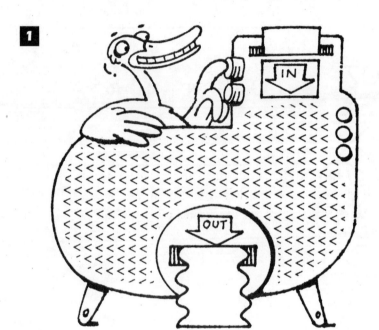

In	3	4	5	7	10
Out	7	8	9		

Rule: _____

2

In	6	7	9	12	10
Out	3	4	6		

Rule: _____

Each machine has a secret rule.
Use cubes and the table to help find each secret rule.
Finish the table.

1

In	2	3	9	6	4
Out	9	10	16		

Rule: _____

2

In	6	7	10	9	12
Out	0	1	4		

Rule: _____

Each machine has a secret rule.
Use cubes and the table to help find each secret rule.
Finish the table.

1

In	5	6	8	10	9
Out	14	15	17		

Rule: _____

2

In	5	7	8	4	10
Out	10	14	16		

Rule: _____

Each machine has a secret rule.

Use cubes and the table to help find each secret rule.

Finish the table.

1

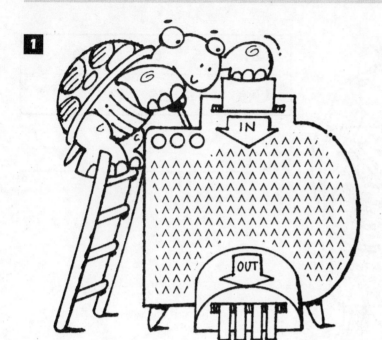

In	3	4	5	6	9
Out	9	12	15		

Rule: _____

2

In	12	8	10	20	18
Out	6	4	5		

Rule: _____

Each machine has a secret rule.
Use the table and a calculator to help find each secret rule.
Finish the table.

1

In	9	10	12	11	15
Out	45	50	60		

Rule: _____

2

In	24	33	18	27	45
Out	8	11	6		

Rule: _____

1 The mice are getting tickets for "Mystery at the Trap." Terry pays for one ticket and gets five tickets! Sara pays for three tickets and gets seven tickets! Rick pays for four tickets and gets eight tickets! Rick scratches his head and says, " What's going on? This IS a mystery!" He watches Molly pay for six tickets. How many tickets will Molly get?

2 Funny things are happening in the Down–Home Hotel. Fred gets on the elevator and presses button 8. The elevator goes to floor 3! Fred presses button 10 and the elevator goes to floor 5! Fred presses button 15, and the elevator goes to floor 10. What's happening? If Fred presses button 21, what floor will the elevator take him to?

3 Polly's Pet Store just received a huge carton from the Fabulous Food Factory. Polly can't believe her eyes when she opens the carton. "I ordered 5 bags of Best Bones, and they sent 25!" she said. "I ordered 3 boxes of Super Seed, and they sent 15 boxes. I ordered 10 buckets of Wonder Worms, and they sent 50 buckets! What's going on?" Polly ordered 20 tubs of Fantastic Flies. How many tubs do you think she got?

Use cubes to solve the problems.

1 There are four more orange fish than blue fish in the fish bowl.
There are five more blue fish than yellow fish.
There are two yellow fish.
How many fish of each color are in the bowl? How many fish in all?

Yellow _____ Blue _____ Orange _____ Total _____

2 There are six more pink fish than green fish in the fish tank.
The number of green fish is the same as the number of red fish.
There are seven red fish.
How many fish of each color are in the tank? How many fish in all?

Red _____ Green _____ Pink _____ Total _____

Use cubes to solve the problems.

1 There are 12 more orange fish than white fish in the fish bowl.
There are three fewer white fish than green fish.
There are eight green fish.
How many fish of each color are in the bowl? How many fish in all?

Green _____ White _____ Orange _____ Total _____

2 There are four fewer green fish than yellow fish in the fish tank.
There are ten more yellow fish than blue fish.
There are six blue fish.
How many fish of each color are in the tank? How many fish in all?

Blue _____ Yellow _____ Green _____ Total _____

Use cubes to solve the problems.

1 The number of orange fish and the number of green fish in the bowl is the same.
There are two fewer green fish than yellow fish.
There are five more yellow fish than white fish.
There are three white fish.
How many fish of each color are in the bowl? How many fish in all?

White _____   Yellow _____   Green _____   Orange _____   Total _____

2 There are four fewer brown fish than blue fish in the fish bowl.
There are eight more blue fish than pink fish.
There is one less pink fish than red fish.
There are four red fish.
How many fish of each color are in the bowl? How many fish in all?

Red _____   Pink _____   Blue _____   Brown _____   Total _____

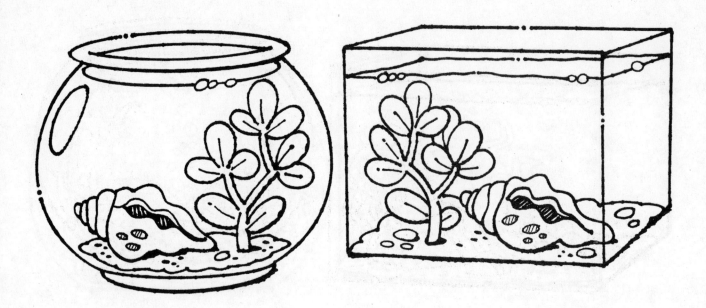

Use cubes to solve the problems.

1 There are two fewer orange fish than black fish in the fish bowl.
There are six more black fish than yellow fish.
There are two times as many yellow fish as red fish.
There are two red fish.
How many fish of each color are in the bowl? How many fish in all?

Red _____ Yellow _____ Black _____ Orange _____ Total _____

2 There are six more white fish than purple fish in the fish tank.
There are four times as many purple fish as blue fish.
There are three fewer blue fish than green fish.
There are five green fish.
How many fish of each color are in the tank? How many fish in all?

Green _____ Blue _____ Purple _____ White _____ Total _____

Use a calculator to solve the problems.

1 There are 16 fewer green fish than blue fish in the fish bowl.
There are three times as many blue fish as red fish.
There are 12 more red fish than white fish.
There are 10 white fish.
How many fish of each color are in the bowl? How many fish in all?

White _____ Red _____ Blue _____ Green _____ Total _____

2 There are 27 fewer brown fish than orange fish in the fish tank.
There are 30 more orange fish than purple fish.
There are four times as many purple fish as yellow fish.
There are 15 yellow fish.
How many fish of each color are in the tank? How many fish in all?

Yellow _____ Purple _____ Orange _____ Brown _____ Total _____

1 The bears were getting takeout at The Cave Fast Food. With great delight they grabbed two times as many bags of honey cakes as bags of berry pies. They got 15 more bags of berry pies than bags of burgers. They grabbed 10 bags of burgers. How many bags of food did the bears take home?

2 Maura took her little sister into the petting zoo. There were three times as many rabbits as goats. There were two fewer goats than sheep. There were three more sheep than pigs. There were six pigs. How many animals were at the petting zoo?

3 On Saturday afternoon Tracy went to the mall with her sister. There were three times as many people in the Pizza Stop as in T-Shirt Madness. There were three fewer people in the T-shirt store than in the Toy Fair. There were two fewer people in the Toy Fair than in the Cookie Cottage. There were eight more people in the Cookie Cottage than in There's Bears. Five people were in There's Bears. How many people were in each store?

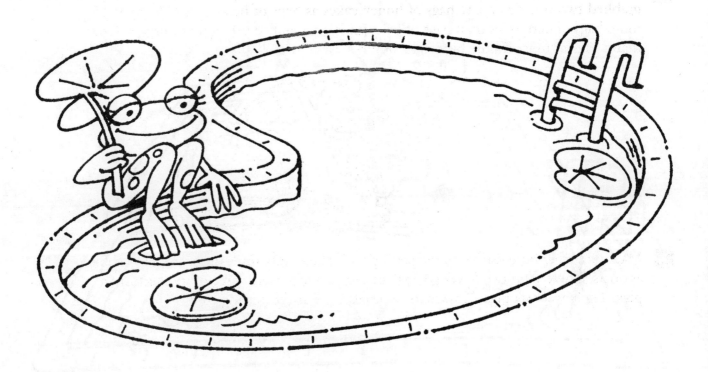

Use cubes to solve the problems.

1 Some pigs and dogs are swimming in the pool.
There are seven animals in the pool.
There is one more pig than dogs.
How many pigs are in the pool? How many dogs?

Pigs _____ Dogs _____

2 Some cats and goats are swimming in the pool.
There are 10 animals in the pool.
There are six more cats than goats.
How many cats are in the pool? How many goats?

Cats _____ Goats _____

Mystery Numbers - 2

Use cubes to solve the problems.

1 Some birds and mice are swimming in the pool.
There are 15 animals in the pool.
There are three fewer birds than mice.
How many birds are in the pool? How many mice?

Birds _____ Mice _____

2 Some rabbits and turtles are swimming in the pool.
There are 20 animals in the pool.
There are four fewer turtles than rabbits.
How many rabbits are in the pool? How many turtles?

Rabbits _____ Turtles _____

Mystery Numbers - 3

Use cubes to solve the problems.

1 Some moles, lizards, and skunks are swimming in the pool.
There are 16 animals in the pool.
There are two more moles than lizards.
There is one less skunk than lizard.
How many moles are in the pool? How many lizards? How many skunks?

Moles _____   Lizards _____   Skunks _____

2 Some possums, raccoons, and snakes are swimming in the pool.
There are 24 animals in the pool.
The number of possums and the number of snakes is the same.
There are six fewer raccoons than snakes.
How many possums are in the pool? How many raccoons?
How many snakes?

Possums _____   Raccoons _____   Snakes _____

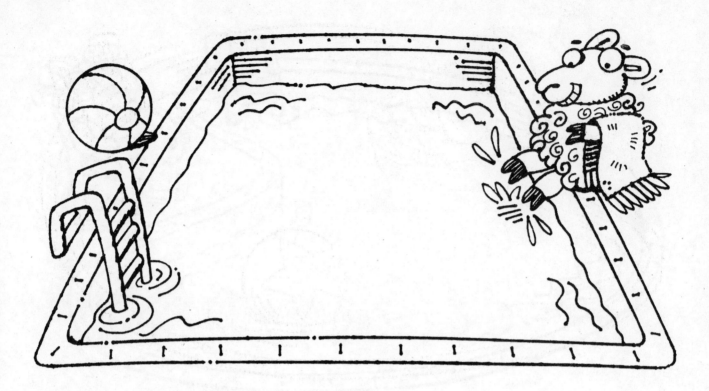

Use cubes to solve the problems.

1 Some dogs, cats, and rabbits are swimming in the pool.
There are 28 animals in the pool.
There are three more dogs than cats.
There are two fewer rabbits than cats.
How many dogs are in the pool? How many cats?
How many rabbits?

Dogs _____ Cats _____ Rabbits _____

2 Some goats, pigs, and turtles are swimming in the pool.
There are 32 animals in the pool.
There are five more goats than pigs.
There are three fewer turtles than pigs.
How many goats are in the pool? How many pigs?
How many turtles?

Goats _____ Pigs _____ Turtles _____

Mystery Numbers - 5

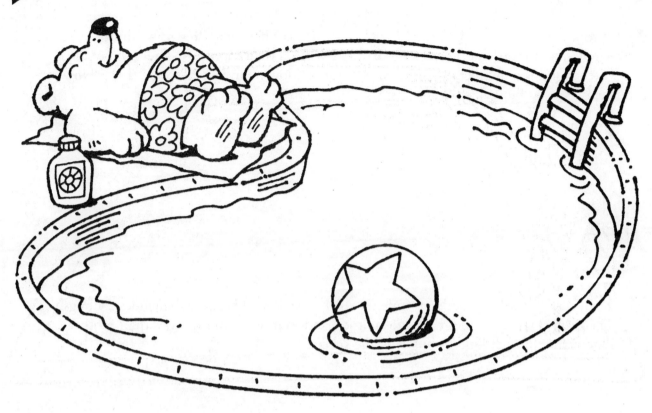

Use a calculator to solve the problems.

1 Some birds, mice, and lizards are swimming in the pool.
There are 55 animals in the pool.
There are eight more mice than birds.
There is one less lizard than birds.
How many birds are in the pool? How many mice?
How many lizards?

Birds _____ Mice _____ Lizards _____

2 Some snakes, possums, and moles are swimming in the pool.
There are 70 animals in the pool.
There are seven more possums than snakes.
There are six fewer moles than snakes.
How many snakes are in the pool?
How many possums? How many moles?

Snakes _____ Possums _____ Moles _____

1 Tyrone opened the door to see 12 trick-or-treaters. They were dressed as ghosts, witches, and monsters. There were six fewer witches than monsters. The number of witches and the number of ghosts was the same. How many witches were there? How many ghosts? How many monsters?

2 There's a big crowd at Birdstop Cafe for the bug special. The special includes 25 bugs! There are three more flies than mosquitoes, and four fewer mosquitoes than moths. How many of each kind of bug is in the special?

3 In her dream, Pilar saw large fuzzy green creatures, small chubby red creatures, and pointy, prickly orange creatures. She counted 30 creatures! There were two more green creatures than red creatures. There were two fewer orange creatures than red creatures. How many creatures of each color were in Pilar's dream?

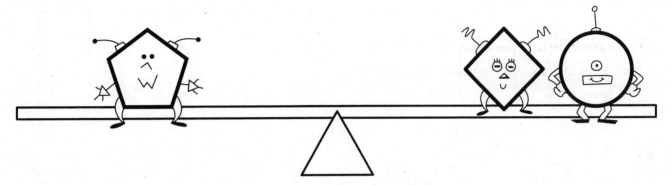

Use cubes to solve the problems.
Find as many solutions as you can.

Rules:

Balance the seesaw.
Robots that are the same have the same weight.
Robots that are different have different weights.
All robots weigh more than zero pounds.

1 If 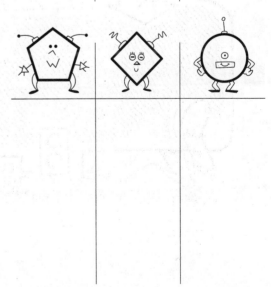 on the seesaw weighs 4 pounds, what could the other robots weigh?

4	1	3
4	3	

2 If on the seesaw weighs 7 pounds, what could the other robots weigh?

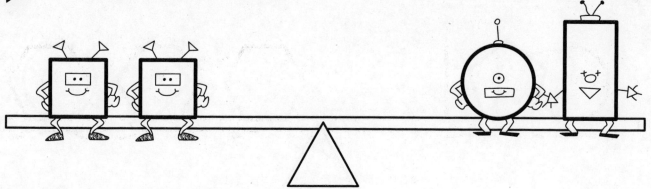

Use cubes to solve the problems.
Find as many solutions as you can.

Rules:

Balance the seesaw.
Robots that are the same have the same weight.
Robots that are different have different weights.
All robots weigh more than zero pounds.

1 If  on the seesaw weighs 3 pounds,
what could the other robots weigh?

2 If on the seesaw weighs 5 pounds,
what could the other robots weigh?

Use cubes to solve the problems.
Find as many solutions as you can.

Rules:

Balance the seesaw.
Robots that are the same have the same weight.
Robots that are different have different weights.
All robots weigh more than zero pounds.

1 If 🤖 on the seesaw weighs 3 pounds, what could the other robots weigh?

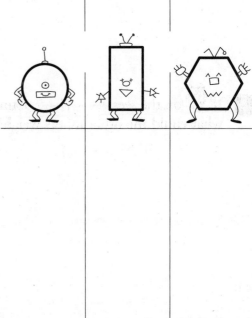

3

2 If 🤖 on the seesaw weighs 4 pounds, what could the other robots weigh?

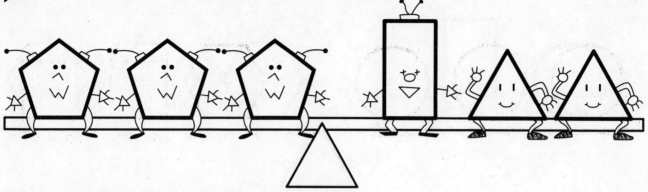

Use cubes to solve the problems.
Find as many solutions as you can.

Rules:

Balance the seesaw.
Robots that are the same have the same weight.
Robots that are different have different weights.
All robots weigh more than zero pounds.

1 If 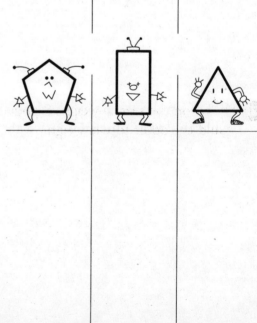 on the seesaw weighs 5 pounds, what could the other robots weigh?

2 If on the seesaw weighs 6 pounds, what could the other robots weigh?

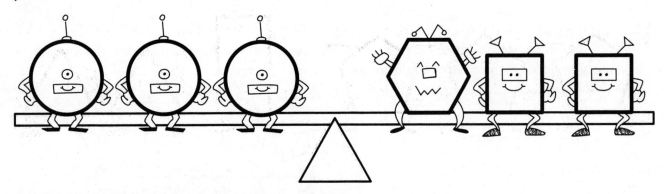

Use a calculator to solve the problems.
Find as many solutions as you can.

Rules:

Balance the seesaw.
Robots that are the same have the same weight.
Robots that are different have different weights.
All robots weigh more than zero pounds.

1 If 🤖 on the seesaw weighs 9 pounds, what could the other robots weigh?

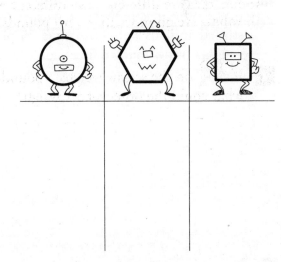

2 If 🤖 on the seesaw weighs 8 pounds, what could the other robots weigh?

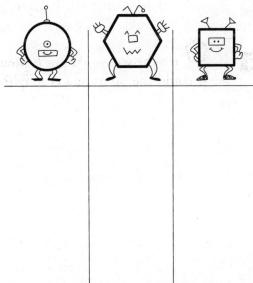

1 Sam the Clown is doing one of his tricks again. He is balancing toys on his head. Each toy clown weighs three ounces. The toy clowns, plane, and robot weigh different amounts. How many ounces could the plane weigh? How many ounces could the robot weigh?

2 Tana put two books in one of her schoolpacks. She put a lunch and two stuffed animals in the other pack. Now the packs weigh the same. Each book weighs 10 ounces. The stuffed animals weigh the same. Books, stuffed animals, and the lunch have different weights. How many ounces could each stuffed animal and the lunch weigh?

3 Tony buys three magnets. Each magnet costs 10 cents. Saburo buys two neon-blue pencils and two troll erasers. He pays the same total amount as Tony does. The pencils cost the same. The erasers cost the same. The prices of pencils, erasers, and magnets are different. What could the prices of each pencil and each eraser be?

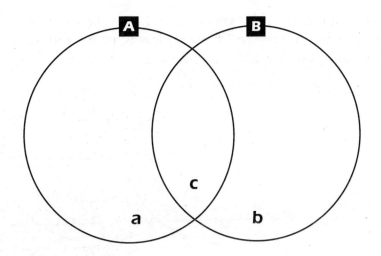

Use cubes to solve the problems.

1 There are pictures of horses in the circles on the wall of the old cave.
There are 8 horses in circle A and 6 horses in circle B.
Two of the horses are in both circles A and B.
How many horses are in the circles?

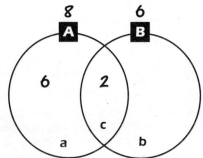

2 There are pictures of cows in the circles on the wall of the old cave.
There are 14 cows in circle A and 11 cows in circle B.
Five of the cows are in both circles A and B.
How many cows are in the circles?

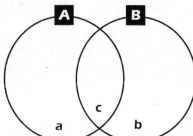

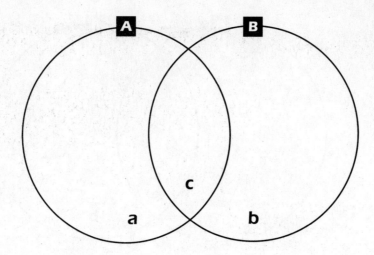

Use cubes to solve the problems.

1 There are pictures of cats in the circles on the wall of the old cave.
There are 17 cats in circle A and 14 cats in circle B.
Seven of the cats are in both circles A and B.
How many cats are in the circles?

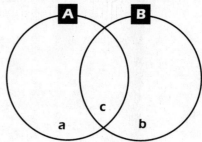

2 There are pictures of dogs in the circles on the wall of the old cave.
There are 20 dogs in circle A and 19 dogs in circle B.
Nine of the dogs are in both circles A and B.
How many dogs are in the circles?

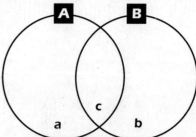

Linking Circles - 3

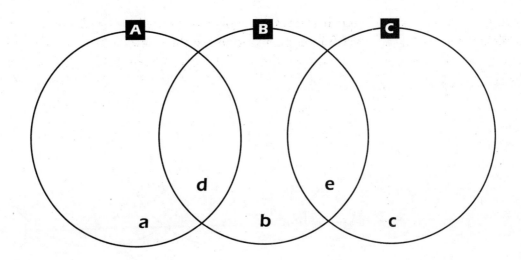

Use cubes to solve the problems.

1 There are pictures of bears in the circles on the wall of the old cave.
There are 8 bears in circle A, 6 bears in circle B, and 8 bears in circle C.
Three of the bears are in both circles A and B.
One of the bears is in both circles B and C.
How many bears are in the circles?

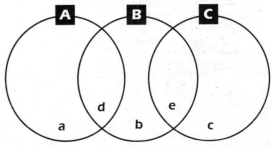

2 There are pictures of deer in the circles on the wall of the old cave.
There are 14 deer in circle A, 16 deer in circle B, and 7 deer in circle C.
Five of the deer are in both circles A and B.
Four of the deer are in both circles B and C.
How many deer are in the circles?

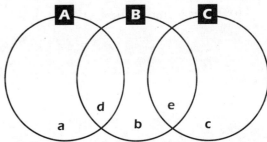

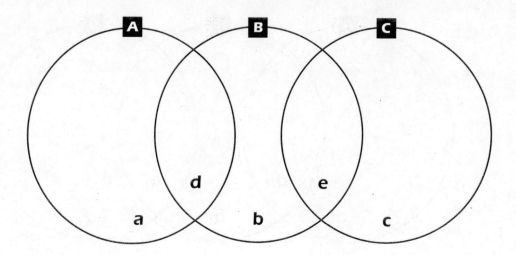

Use cubes to solve the problems.

1 There are pictures of birds in the circles on the wall of the old cave.
There are 12 birds in circle A, 14 birds in circle B, and 9 birds in circle C.
Seven of the birds are in both circles A and B.
Three of the birds are in both circles B and C.
How many birds are in the circles?

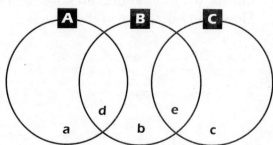

2 There are pictures of snakes in the circles on the wall of the old cave.
There are 10 snakes in circle A, 20 snakes in circle B, and 13 snakes in circle C.
Six of the snakes are in both circles A and B.
Five of the snakes are in both circles B and C.
How many snakes are in the circles?

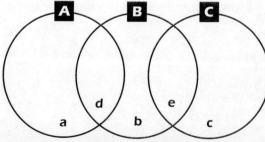

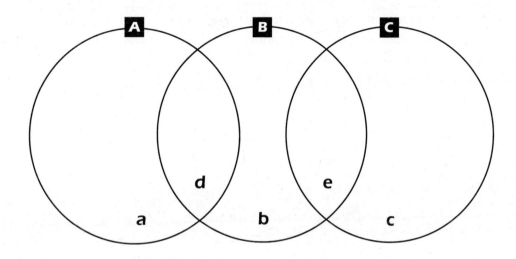

Use a calculator to solve the problems.

1 There are pictures of horses in the circles on the wall of the old cave.
There are 25 horses in circle A, 46 horses in circle B, and 40 horses in circle C.
Fifteen of the horses are in both circles A and B.
Eleven of the horses are in both circles B and C.
How many horses are in the circles?

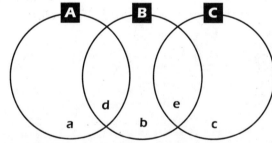

2 There are pictures of cows in the circles on the wall of the old cave.
There are 42 cows in circle A, 71 cows in circle B, and 45 cows in circle C.
Twelve of the cows are in both circles A and B.
Seventeen of the cows are in both circles B and C.
How many cows are in the circles?

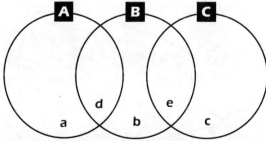

1 The children played games and ate hamburgers, hot dogs, and potato salad at the Fourth-of-July Picnic. Twenty-seven children ate hamburgers, and 25 children ate hot dogs. Twelve of these children ate both hamburgers and hot dogs. How many children were at the picnic?

2 Mary did a survey to find out if people had tasted her three favorite cereals. She found that 10 people had tasted Jiffy Jumbles, 18 people had tasted Critter Chips, and eight people had tasted Teddy Toasties. There were seven people who had tasted Jiffy Jumbles and Critter Chips, and two people who had tasted Critter Chips and Teddy Toasties. How many people took part in Mary's survey?

3 The spaceship X-ton offered free trips to Numba, Tronex, and Sentra. Twenty-four robotons visited Numba, 34 robotons visited Tronex, and 23 robotons visited Sentra. Fourteen of these robotons visited both Numba and Tronex, and 11 robotons visited both Tronex and Sentra. How many robotons took advantage of the free trips on X-ton?

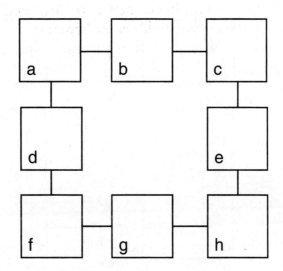

Cut out eight small squares of paper. Number them 1 through 8.

Use the cutouts and a list to solve each puzzle.

1 Use the numbers 1 through 8. List the ways to make the sum of 12 using three different addends. Then solve the puzzle. The sum of the numbers on each side of the square must be 12. Put a different number in each space.

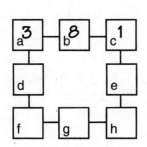

Sum of 12

8 + 3 + 1 = 12

7 + 4 + 1 = 12

2 Use the numbers 1 through 8. List the ways to make the sum of 14 using three different addends. Then solve the puzzle. The sum of the numbers on each side of the square must be 14. Put a different number in each space.

Sum of 14

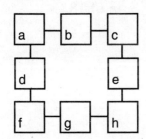

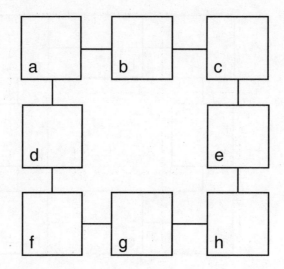

Cut out eight small squares of paper. Number them 2 through 9.

Use the cutouts and a list to solve each puzzle.

1 Use the numbers 2 through 9. List the ways to make the sum of 16 using three different addends. Then solve the puzzle. The sum of the numbers on each side of the square must be 16. Put a different number in each space.

<u>Sum of 16</u>

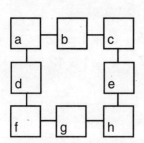

2 Use the numbers 2 through 9. List the ways to make the sum of 18 using three different addends. Then solve the puzzle. The sum of the numbers on each side of the square must be 18. Put a different number in each space.

<u>Sum of 18</u>

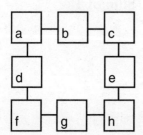

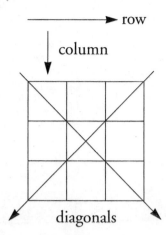

row

column

diagonals

a	b	c
d	e	f
g	h	i

Cut out ten small squares of paper. Number them 1 through 10.

Use the cutouts and a list to solve each puzzle.

1 Use the numbers 1 through 9. List the ways to make the sum of 15 using three different addends. Then solve the puzzle. The sum of the numbers in each row, column, and diagonal must be 15. Put a different number in each space.

<u>Sum of 15</u>

a	b	c
d	e	f
g	h	i

2 Use the numbers 2 through 10. List the ways to make the sum of 18 using three different addends. Then solve the puzzle. The sum of the numbers in each row, column, and diagonal must be 18. Put a different number in each space.

<u>Sum of 18</u>

a	b	c
d	e	f
g	h	i

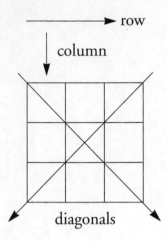

row

column

diagonals

a	b	c
d	e	f
g	h	i

Cut out 13 small squares of paper. Number them 0 through 12.

Use the cutouts and a list to solve each puzzle.

1 Use the numbers 0 through 8. List the ways to make the sum of 12 using three different addends. Then solve the puzzle. The sum of the numbers in each row, column, and diagonal must be 12. Put a different number in each space.

Sum of 12

a	b	c
d	e	f
g	h	i

2 Use the numbers 2 through 12. List the ways to make the sum of 21 using three different addends. Then solve the puzzle. The sum of the numbers in each row, column, and diagonal must be 21. Put a different number in each space.

Sum of 21

a	b	c
d	e	f
g	h	i

Square Puzzles - 5

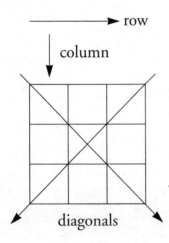

row

column

diagonals

a	b	c
d	e	f
g	h	i

Use a calculator to solve the puzzles.

1 Use any number from 1 through 21. The sum of the numbers in each row, column, and diagonal is 33. Find a different number for each space.

a	b	c
d	e	f
g	h	i

2 Use any number from 5 through 40. The sum of the numbers in each row, column, and diagonal is 75. Find a different number for each space.

a	b	c
d	e	f
g	h	i

1 It is called the Twenties Mystery House. The house has 20 tiny rooms and 20 tiny doors. There is a square fence around the house. The fence has eight posts. The posts are numbered 3 through 10.

The sum of the numbers on each side of the fence is 20. How could each post be numbered?

2 Ben told his brother and sister that if they could solve his puzzle, he would wash the dishes for a week. "It's a deal," they said. Ben drew this puzzle:

He said they could use any of the numbers from 3 through 13. But they had to put a different number in each space. The sum of the numbers in each row, column, and diagonal had to be 24. They did it! Ben had to wash the dishes for a week. How do you think they solved the puzzle?

3 The treasure room door is locked. Molly and Mark want to go inside. To unlock the door, they have to enter numbers in this square a certain way.

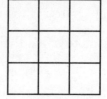

The sum of the numbers in each row, column, and diagonal must be 45. They can only use the numbers 11 through 19. Each space must have a different number. What is one way they could unlock the door?

Story Problems - 1

1 The fourth-grade students set up a booth at the Fantastic Food Fair on Saturday. They hung up their Hot Popcorn sign and started popping the corn. People followed their noses to the booth! The students sold 13 bags of popcorn in the first hour, 19 bags in the second hour, 25 in the third hour, and 31 in the fourth hour. If people keep buying like that, how many bags will the students sell in the eighth hour?

2 Mimi and Nate are making creatures at the Create-a-Critter factory. Mimi is making alligoats and Nate is making crocodogs. They pack 4 alligoats and 8 crocodogs in each box. There are 72 creatures in boxes, ready to be shipped. How many alligoats and crocodogs have Mimi and Nate made?

3 Karl and Laura were building a sand castle with a huge moat and three towers. On this warm summer day there were 10 fewer people playing ball than there were swimming. There were two times as many people swimming as there were building sand castles. There were five more people building sand castles than there were on surfboards. There were eight people on surfboards. How many people were playing ball, building sand castles, swimming, and riding surfboards?

1 Between four o'clock and five o'clock 43 people used the city pool. There were four times as many people taking swimming lessons as diving lessons. There were five fewer people taking diving lessons than were playing water polo. There were two more people playing water polo than were taking a water safety lesson. There were eight people taking a water safety class. How many people did each activity?

2 The cellar steps of the old Grimes house had treasure hidden under them. When the house was torn down, six bags of coins and five bags of bills were discovered under each step. If 121 bags of money were found under the steps, how many bags were filled with coins and how many were filled with bills?

3 Bear-Wear Bonanza is having a terrific sale this week! Barry's family bought 5 pairs of shoes and left the store with 10 pairs. Cathy's family bought 8 T-shirts and went home with 16! Dana's family bought 4 pairs of jeans and left the store with 8 pairs! What's happening at Bear-Wear Bonanza? If Eli's family buys 10 pairs of socks, how many pairs of socks will they get?

1 The New Improved Corn Crispies are almost flying out the door of Dora's Deli! Dora can't keep the bags on the shelves! She sold 10 bags in the first hour, 20 bags in the second hour, 30 bags in the third hour, and 40 bags in the fourth hour. If the pattern continues, how many bags of Corn Crispies will Dora sell all together in five hours?

2 Professor Digger dug up an old pot. Under all the layers of dirt and dust, he could see a square. In the square, he could see three rows of numbers. There were three numbers in each row. In the top row he saw 12, 27, and 6. When he washed off all the dirt, he could see all nine numbers. Each number was different. He saw a 3 and five more numbers that were between 3 and 27. The sum of the numbers in each row, column, and diagonal was the same. What were the other five numbers?

3 Angelina took her dog to play in the park. There were 19 dogs leaping and running in circles on the grass. There were two more brown dogs than black dogs. There were six fewer white dogs than brown dogs. How many dogs of each color were there?

1 Marco is riding the subway with his Dad. In Marco's car there are twice as many people talking as listening to headphones. There are five fewer people listening to headphones than reading. There are six more people reading than sleeping. There are six people sleeping. How many people are in Marco's subway car?

2 Kelly starts to play Robo-Scrunchers on the computer. She clicks on the number 18, and 9 robots march onto the screen. She clicks on 50, and 25 robots race across the screen. She clicks on 36, and 18 robots fly across the screen. She clicks 42, and 21 robots swim past her eyes. If she clicks on the number 26, how many robots will appear on the screen?

3 The 36 frogs were lined up for the great Leapoff. Each team was wearing a different-colored T-shirt. There were two more blue shirts than yellow shirts. There were two more yellow shirts than red shirts. There were two fewer orange shirts than red shirts. How many frogs were on each team?

1 Gail and her mom are buying fruit at the market. Gail puts a melon on the scale. It weighs 15 ounces. Then Gail's mom chooses two apples and one pear. The apples and pear together weigh the same as the melon. The two apples weigh the same. The pear weighs a different amount than an apple. How many ounces could each apple and the pear weigh?

2 Graciela and Danny knew that the key to the combination of the old safe was the number 24. If they set the numbers on each side of the square so that they had a sum of 24, then the safe would open! If they used the numbers 4 through 11 for the eight numbers, how could they have arranged the numbers?

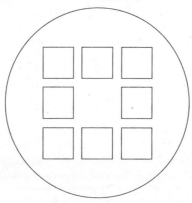

3 Garth asked third- and fourth-grade students whether they liked to play soccer or basketball. Thirty students said they liked to play soccer and 25 students said that they liked to play basketball. Twelve of these students said they liked to play both soccer and basketball. How many students did Garth talk to?

1 Berta and Carrie have to make 36 favors for a party. So far, they have made 14 favors with green ribbons, 20 favors with orange ribbons, and 11 favors with yellow ribbons. Six of these favors have both orange and green ribbons; five of the favors have both orange and yellow ribbons. How many favors do they have left to make?

2 Nina and Luis paid the same amount. Nina bought one bag of Nutty Nuggets at $0.25. Luis bought one Grand Slam Bar and two boxes of DinoCrunches. If a Grand Slam Bar and a box of DinoCrunches cost different amounts, what could their prices be?

3 Gina lived near a busy airport. One night she looked up and counted 14 bright lights in the sky. Some were moving faster than others. She saw two more stars than planes in the sky. How many stars and how many planes did she see?